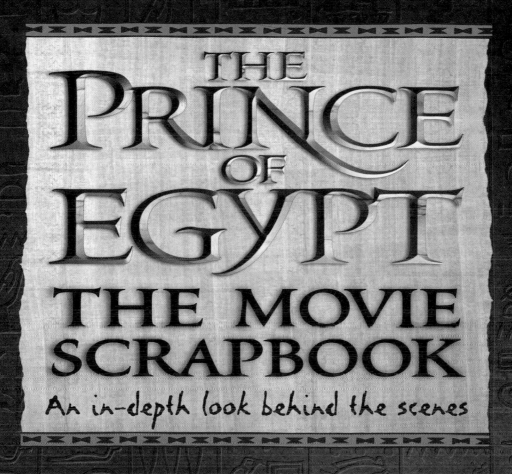

THE PRINCE OF EGYPT

THE MOVIE SCRAPBOOK

An in-depth look behind the scenes

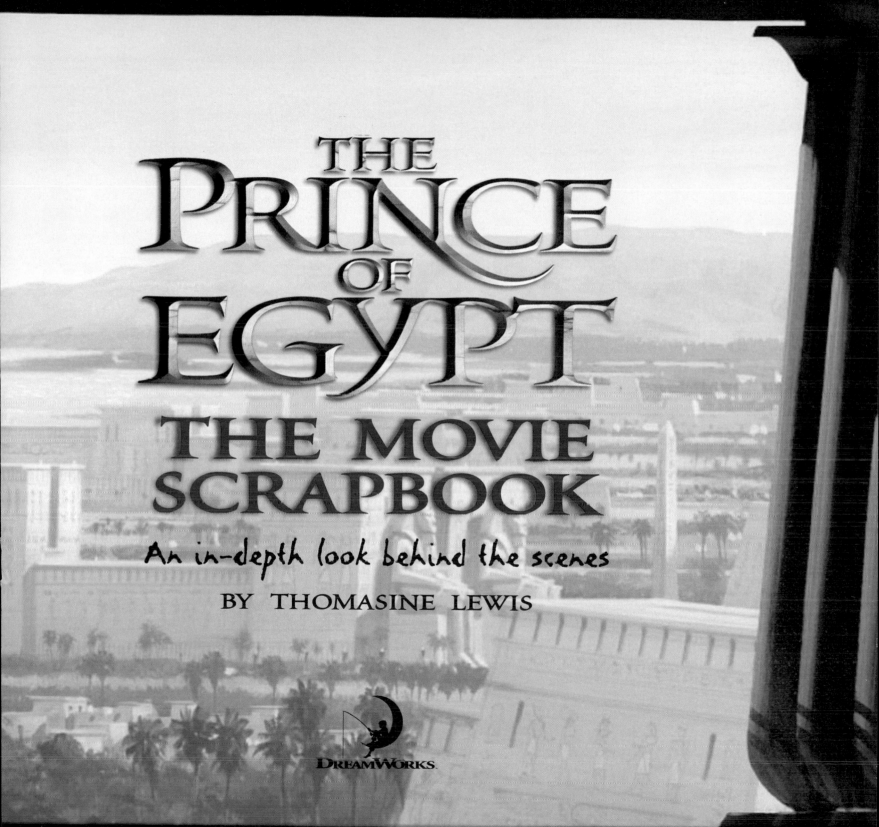

THE PRINCE OF EGYPT

THE MOVIE SCRAPBOOK

An in-depth look behind the scenes

BY THOMASINE LEWIS

DreamWorks

Contents

INTRODUCTION

I f you think building the pyramids was a monumental task, here's another one: Imagine taking four hundred artists from twenty-six different countries and asking them to spend three and a half years of their lives "building" a movie. And not just *any* movie—one about God, Moses, and miracles.

The DreamWorks studio chiefs, from left: Steven Spielberg, Jeffrey Katzenberg, and David Geffen.

So how did *The Prince of Egypt* come to be? Steven Spielberg, Jeffrey Katzenberg, and David Geffen were discussing what elements make a great animated movie.

Jeffrey said, "It's got to be a fantastic story . . . one that would be hard to tell in *live action*. One that is epic and grand."

Steven paused, then said, "You mean as epic and grand as the story of Moses and the Ten Commandments?"

That's *exactly* what Jeffrey meant. Their new movie studio should base its first animated movie on the life of Moses. But, Steven wondered, could they really pull this off? After all, most animated movies were fairy tales for young children. There had never been an attempt to create an animated movie about an epic adventure this grand—with biblical origins that were deeply meaningful to many people.

"It's got all the elements," Jeffrey argued convincingly. "There's a strong villain and hero. The story is larger-than-life and has a moral that speaks to all ages! It's *perfect*."

So the idea was hatched. After the DreamWorks movie studio was established, the writers produced the first draft of the script. Storyboard artists began laying out the movie's opening scenes. And the voices were cast—a stunning array of talent: Michelle Pfeiffer, Val Kilmer, Sandra Bullock, Ralph Fiennes, Jeff Goldblum, Patrick Stewart, Steve Martin, Martin Short, Danny Glover, Helen Mirren. One by one, these top stars entered a studio and recorded their parts.

Over the next two and a half years, animators and other artists brought the script and celebrities' voices to life with their drawings. The producers and directors oversaw every scene. The song composer and lyricist spent weeks in a recording studio. The special-effects artists created more special effects than any animated movie ever before, including a monumental climax: the parting of the Red Sea, a scene that took two years to complete.

"It was such an exciting opportunity," Jeffrey Katzenberg recalled. "A great story . . . great characters . . .

even miracles that we could animate. With this story, we knew we could take animation in a completely new direction."

Join us on this exclusive behind-the-scenes journey into how *The Prince of Egypt* was made. Meet the artists, producers, directors, songwriters, and storytellers. Discover each step in the creation of animation movie magic. Learn fascinating trivia and how to draw *The Prince of Egypt* characters. Lift the curtain and find out how the greatest story ever told was made into a groundbreaking animated movie.

 DreamWorks SKG is Hollywood's first new, major studio in more than fifty years.

THE STORY OF THE FILM

"My son, I have nothing I can give but this chance that you may live." With these words, a Hebrew mother puts her baby son in a basket and sets it afloat on the Nile River.

After a turbulent journey, the basket comes to rest in the calm waters near the Royal Palace. The Pharaoh's wife

"My son, I have nothing I can give but this chance that you may live."

finds the infant wrapped in blankets, unharmed. She adopts the baby as her own and names him Moses.

Moses grows up as Egyptian royalty—a Prince —and develops a deep friendship with the Queen's son, Rameses, who Moses believes is his real brother. As a young man, Moses is carefree

and adventurous, while Rameses is more serious and cautious, for he is next in line to take over Pharaoh Seti's throne and become the ruler of the kingdom.

Moses is proud of Rameses' future and protects his

brother when Pharaoh Seti disciplines them for their boyhood pranks. Then one night, an incident sets off a chain of events that unrav-

els Moses' world. At a banquet, the palace magicians, Hotep and Huy, present Rameses with a gift, a Midianite woman named Tzipporah. Rameses gives Tzipporah to Moses, but she escapes to the Hebrew settlement of Goshen. Moses follows her. In Goshen, he loses Tzipporah, but encounters his real

sister and brother, the Hebrew slaves Miriam and Aaron.

Miriam reveals to Moses the truth of his birth: He is really the son of a Hebrew slave. Moses refuses to believe her and runs back to the palace. Exhausted, he falls asleep and has a nightmare in which babies are torn from their mothers' arms and

thrown into a river filled with crocodiles. When Moses wakes up, he is horrified to find hieroglyphs on the palace walls that depict the images that appeared in his dream.

Moses confronts Pharaoh Seti, who tries to explain: "The Hebrews grew too numerous. They might have risen against us." Moses cannot believe what he's hearing. "Sometimes for the greater good, sacrifices must be made," his father continues. Then he adds, "They were only slaves."

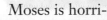

Moses is horrified and tormented. He is not the prince he thought he was, and he is now beginning to see the slaves as real people . . . *his* people. The morning after his discovery, Moses and Rameses go to the site of a new temple where Moses sees for the first time the brutal lives of the Hebrews. When a taskmaster strikes an elderly slave, Moses tries to defend the old man and ends up killing the guard. "I will make it so it never happened," Rameses assures him. But Moses is stunned by what he's done, and flees Egypt.

He spends days aimlessly wandering the desert before coming to a Midianite village, where he again meets Tzipporah. Her father, Jethro, is the high priest of Midian. He welcomes Moses into their tribe. As the years pass, Moses builds a life as a shepherd. He falls in love with Tzipporah and they marry.

One day, when Moses is out with his sheep, he comes across a small bush burning brightly—yet the bush seems untouched by the fire. Moses extends his staff into the flames, but the staff is unaffected. He puts his hand into the fire, and it, too, is unharmed. Suddenly, a gentle voice echoes around him and calls his name. "I am the God of your ancestors," the voice reveals. God commands Moses to return to Egypt and free the Hebrew slaves.

Inspired by God's directive, Moses and Tzipporah travel to Egypt and find that Pharaoh Seti has died, and Rameses is now pharaoh. Moses tells his brother about God's command, but Rameses refuses to let the Hebrews leave Egypt. In fact, the

request angers Rameses, and he doubles the slaves' workload.

Moses tries to convince Rameses of God's power, but Rameses is unimpressed, even after he sees the Nile River turn to blood. Moses warns that God will inflict more terrible plagues on Egypt. Rameses ignores this warning, and one by one, the plagues devastate the land of Egypt. The last plague kills Rameses' own young son. Defeated, Rameses tells Moses, "You and your people have my permission to go."

Moses leads the Hebrews out of Egypt, with much rejoicing, but as they reach the shores of the Red Sea, they see Rameses' army coming after them. The Hebrews are trapped. Moses calls to God, and the mighty Red Sea parts, allowing the Hebrews to safely cross. The waters crash down on the pursuing army.

Safe on the far shore, the Hebrews celebrate their newfound freedom.

Three months later, Moses stands before his people at Mount Sinai and delivers the Ten Commandments, handed down by God.

"There can be miracles when you believe."

IN THE BEGINNING

Early on, Jeffrey Katzenberg admitted that *The Prince of Egypt* was an "extremely ambitious movie that takes on an extraordinary story." This meant Jeffrey and Steven Spielberg needed to select a special group of experienced producers and directors.

For *The Prince of Egypt*, they chose two producers—Penney Finkelman Cox and Sandra Rabins—and three directors—Brenda Chapman, Steve Hickner, and Simon Wells.

The producers oversaw the development, production, and post production of the film. They supervised the hiring of the cast and crew, then made sure the story was followed, deadlines were met, and a budget was adhered to.

Penney said the first thing the producers and directors did was have "a million story meetings. We had a staff writer and a team of story artists who helped us sculpt the story," she explained. "We couldn't just read the Bible. We had to read what all the great minds have written. We had to go to other sources—theologians, historians, Egyptologists—to really gain a depth of understanding that would allow us not to simplify the story but to bring it many layers of richness."

And this was just the *beginning*.

As the story was being developed, actors were picked to do the characters' voices. Sandy explained, "We sat in a room and listened to voices on tape, not knowing, necessarily, who the actor or actress was. We tried to decide which voices felt best to us based on our sense of the character and the character art. In many cases, the characters had to age—as Moses did from age eighteen to

From the top: Producers Sandra Rabins and Penney Finkelman Cox, Directors Brenda Chapman, Steve Hickner, and Simon Wells.

The final soundtrack recording studio in London.

Penney Finkelman Cox, Simon Wells, Jeffrey Katzenberg, Brenda Chapman, and Steve Hickner supervise the recording.

Danny Glover recording the voice of Jethro.

forty—so we needed people who had the flexibility to do a young and an older voice. When we came to a decision, we turned the voice tape over to an animator who matched it to a piece of animation. If the voice and animation meshed, we took the next step and talked to the actors themselves. We got lucky. All the people we wanted were glad to participate, and we ended up with a dream cast."

The directors were the creative leaders, responsible for everything from camera angles and color choices to supervising the writers, animators, and composers.

All three directors have different talents. Brenda's strength is in storytelling, because her background is writing. Simon is an animator turned director, so he paid special attention to the drawings and layout. And Steve has worked in both the production and art departments, which has allowed him an understanding of all the subtleties and possibilities of animation. But they *all* were responsible for the performances—the recorded voices and animated characters. As Penney explained: "We didn't divide the directors up. Everyone worked together and constantly communicated about what the others were doing."

13

DEVELOPING THE STORY

At the core of every great movie is a great script. For *The Prince of Egypt*, the story team had the daunting task of creating a script based on the life of Moses—a powerful, moral story of freedom and deliverance. The story has the four most essential components of a top-notch narrative: drama, adventure, romance, and even some comedy.

The drama of the brothers, Moses and Rameses, who are destined to become enemies, struck a powerful emotional chord. "It's painful," said Lorna Cook, one of the two heads of story. "There's a sadness between them when they have to go their separate ways. How would you feel if you were losing your brother?"

"But we didn't want to convey the feeling that all Egyptians are bad and all Hebrews are good," insisted Lorna's partner, head of story Kelly Asbury. "We wanted to show that they are all humans with different belief systems that are not good or bad—it's what they believe."

The Prince of Egypt is also an adventure story. "I think you can find the same themes in many classic films, from *Star Wars* to *Raiders of the Lost Ark*, which are about a central figure who believes in the ultimate truth, follows

his heart, and conquers his enemy," said Kelly. "After Moses' encounter with God at the burning bush, he embarks on a mission to lead the slaves out of Egypt. It's not something he asked for, but he went for it—sometimes with a lot of fear and sadness."

The relationship between Tzipporah and Moses adds a romance component to the story.

Because the movie is based in realism, the last component, comedy, is not derived from talking animal sidekicks and the slapstick usually found in animated movies. Instead, the humor is rooted in real-life scenarios, like the

> *The Prince of Egypt* **is made up of approximately 136,000 frames, making up a total of 8,540 feet of film.**

Drawings from the storyboards, showing the chariot race.

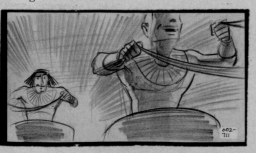

witty banter and pranks of the young Moses and Rameses and the over-the-top arrogance and fussiness of the magicians Hotep and Huy.

With a lot of material and a limited amount of screen time, the story of *The Prince of Egypt* was not easy to tell. The storytellers chose to leave some aspects of the Bible story out of the movie. For instance, they didn't show Moses' relationship with his natural mother—she doesn't appear again in the film after she puts baby Moses in the basket on the Nile, although in the Bible she was his wet nurse. In addition, there is no mention of Moses' sons, but in the Bible, he had two. The storytellers also had to find creative ways to condense major events. "We didn't

"...sometimes for the greater good, sacrifices must be made."

have a lot of time to show Moses going from being a prince in Egypt to a shepherd in Midian," Kelly cited as an example. "So we used a song, 'Through Heaven's Eyes,' to show his transformation."

And since the story of Moses is a part of many of the world's religions, the storytellers were responsible for telling the story in a way that was sensitive to many faiths. "We had hundreds of leaders from various religious communities—clergy and biblical scholars—work with us on the film," said Lorna. Besides working with

these expert consultants and advisers, the story team, directors, and producers read hundreds of books, including the Bible and other religious documents, and took a two-week fact-finding trip to Egypt where they experienced firsthand the grandeur of the pyramids and the vastness of the desert. Still, changes were made to the traditional biblical story.

Lorna Cook and Kelly Asbury discuss the storyboard.

"For instance," Kelly explained, "we had the Queen find the baby Moses, rather than the daughter of Pharaoh, as in the Bible. And a pharaoh probably would have had many more children than we represent in the film. [Rameses, in fact, had more than one hundred children.] But we chose to keep it simple, focus on the two brothers, and have Moses raised in the palace as a prince."

There were other changes. "In the Bible, Aaron, Moses' brother, is basically the mouthpiece for Moses," Lorna explained. "We couldn't portray him that way in our story because it would have taken too much away from Moses. So Aaron became the skeptic who represents the doubt and cynicism of the Hebrews."

The most interesting character to develop, Kelly revealed, was Rameses. "Here he is, raised in privilege, now the ruler of Egypt, and he's ultimately faced by his brother, who he loves most in the world. Should he listen to his brother or remain true to his heritage and honor? Rameses goes through an emotional struggle just as strongly as Moses does."

After the characters and the basic framework of the story were established, the heads of story, with the producers and directors, went to work mapping out the film. They managed a staff of artists and a writer, who worked together to create the visuals and the dialogue for the story.

Selected illustrations representing the main events in the story were posted on outline boards. By showing how the film breaks down into its key moments, the outline boards give a very visual, easy-to-follow picture of the story of the film.

Next the storyboards were created: a series of black-

and-white drawings that include every scene and give a detailed look at the story. These drawings are organized into sequences, or groups of scenes that tell a chunk of the story. For instance, the prologue, which shows baby Moses' turbulent journey down the Nile in a basket, is the first sequence in the film. Sound effects and camera movements were also noted on the storyboards, even at this early stage.

The storyboard and outline board were valuable tools for planning. All of the work that followed, whether music or animation, referred back to these visual representations of the story.

13.5 MOSES REVILED

MOSES walks through a work site, witnessing the suffering of the HEBREWS, who angrily ridicule their would-be deliverer and throw mud at him. MIRIAM intervenes and tells MOSES he must have faith and not give up. He decides to confront RAMESES again.

15. NILE TO BLOOD

MOSES, seeing RAMESES sailing down the Nile, shouts at him to let his people go. RAMESES orders him seized, and as the GUARDS start to enter the water, MOSES touches his staff to the Nile and turns it to blood.

15.5 THE RALLY

AARON is disappointed at MOSES' failure to sway RAMESES: "I guess that's the end of that." MOSES, steadfast in his faith, replies: "No, Aaron, it's just beginning."

16. THE PLAGUES

MOSES summons 8 more PLAGUES (flies, frogs, locusts, etc.). Egypt's might diminishes as the power of MOSES and the HEBREW GOD grows throughout the land. Yet RAMESES will not back down.

A section of the outline board shows the artwork and corresponding description for each of four sequences.

Larger than Life

Moses and Rameses both claim a great place in history. Often they are presented as epic, heroic figures who are larger than life, but *The Prince of Egypt* humanizes them, so we can understand them as real people. Here is some background information from biblical and historical sources.

MOSES

BORN: thirteenth century B.C. (also written B.C.E., meaning "before the common era").

INTERESTING FACT: The name "Moses" comes from a Hebrew word meaning "to draw out," appropriate since Moses was drawn out of the Nile River.

PARENTS: His father was Amram, and his mother was Yocheved. She hid Moses from the Egyptians for three months before placing him in a basket in the river to save his life.

MARRIED: Tzipporah.

CHILDREN: Two sons, Gershom and Eliezer.

HISTORICAL ACCOMPLISHMENTS: He led the Hebrews out of Egypt, parted the Red Sea, and received the Ten Commandments from God.

AGE AT DEATH: 120!

CIRCUMSTANCE AT DEATH: Right before Moses died, God let him see the Promised Land (now Israel), but told him he wouldn't be able to go there.

BURIED: In a valley of the land of Moab, opposite Beth-peor, which today is in Jordan.

RAMESES

BORN: thirteenth century B.C.

ALSO KNOWN AS: Rameses the Great, Rameses II, and Pi-Rameses.

PARENTS: Pharaoh Seti I and Queen Nefari.

LENGTH OF REIGN: sixty-seven years.

MARRIED: He had many wives, but his favorite was Nefertari.

CHILDREN: He had around one hundred sons and fifty daughters. His successor, Ramescs III, was born to his wife Isinofre.

HISTORICAL ACCOMPLISHMENTS: He built his own city, Pi-Ramesse, known for its exquisite beauty and architecture. He also built the temple to Osiris, and he recaptured lands that his father had lost, including present-day Syria, Israel, Jordan, and Lebanon.

BURIED: Rameses was mummified, and the mummy is currently in the Egyptian Museum in Cairo, Egypt. He appears to have died of old age.

MEET THE CAST

VAL KILMER
AS MOSES

He's played larger-than life fictional characters—
Batman in *Batman Forever* and a spy in *The Saint*.
Now Val has tackled one of history's most important
figures: Moses. Val's movie credits include *Top Gun* and
The Doors, in which he played rock star Jim Morrison.

"Let my people go."

RALPH FIENNES
AS RAMESES

"I am the morning and evening star! I am Pharaoh!"

Ralph Fiennes (pronounced "Rafe Fines") has a flair for accents. In *Schindler's List* (his first big movie, directed by Steven Spielberg), he was so convincing as the Nazi colonel, some people thought he really was German. In *Quiz Show*, Ralph played an American with a New England inflection. In the Oscar-winning movie *The English Patient*, this British actor played a Hungarian posing as an Englishman. You can also see Ralph in *The Avengers*.

MICHELLE PFEIFFER
AS TZIPPORAH, MOSES' WIFE

Michelle also starred in a Batman movie—she was Catwoman in *Batman Returns*. Besides doing her own singing in *The Prince of Egypt*, she sang and played starring roles in *Grease 2* and *The Fabulous Baker Boys*, a film that won her an Academy Award nomination. Michelle's movie credits also include *Dangerous Minds* and *Up Close and Personal*.

"I demand you set me free!"

21

SANDRA BULLOCK
AS MIRIAM, MOSES' SISTER

She was the crafty bus driver in *Speed* and also starred in *The Net* and *While You Were Sleeping*. Who wouldn't want a sister like Sandra? She's a bubbly person, so Miriam's animator made the character more lively than the others. He also said he put Sandra's sweetness into Miriam's character.

"I know who you are! And you are not a Prince of Egypt!"

JEFF GOLDBLUM
AS AARON, MOSES' BROTHER

As Dr. Ian Malcolm, Jeff survived dinosaur attacks twice: in *Jurassic Park* and *The Lost World*. He also saved the world in *Independence Day*. Aaron's animator noticed that Jeff uses his hands a lot when he speaks, and decided to make that one of Aaron's mannerisms.

"God? When did God start caring about any of us?"

PATRICK STEWART
AS THE PHARAOH SETI

When you need someone to play a powerful ruler, who do you turn to? The producers and directors selected Patrick, who not only played the captain on *Star Trek: The Next Generation* but is also a prominent Shakespearean actor. He has played King Henry in *Henry V*, the title role in *Titus Andronicus*, and Prospero in *The Tempest*.

"They were only slaves."

HELEN MIRREN
AS THE QUEEN

Helen seems destined for queendom—she played Queen Charlotte in the movie *The Madness of King George* and is considered one of the queens of theater in her homeland, England. When the animator first heard Helen's voice, he said he got chills and actually fell in love with it.

"You are our son and we love you."

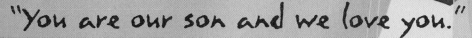

"You're playing with the big boys now."

STEVE MARTIN AS HOTEP   MARTIN SHORT AS HUY

These actors starred together in *The Three Amigos* and *Father of the Bride*, and now they are reunited as the magicians in *The Prince of Egypt*. Steve plays the grumpy chubby magician and Martin plays the shy thin one. But in the studio, everyone said Steve was quiet and Martin was outgoing, constantly cracking jokes.

DANNY GLOVER
AS JETHRO, TZIPPORAH'S FATHER

Danny is probably best known for the *Lethal Weapon* movies. Jethro's animator said he used Danny's expressive smile for the character. Jethro's singing voice was performed by Broadway star Brian Stokes Mitchell.

"You have been sent as a blessing."

THE MUSIC

Music is so important to an animated film that it becomes one of the stars. It sets moods—an uplifting tune can make a scene more joyous, a soulful one can bring an audience to tears. A song can enhance the emotional power of the dialogue or set the mood for a sequence that tells a vital part of the story.

Two of the music industry's leading talents, both Academy Award winners, spent almost four years creating the soundtrack for *The Prince of Egypt*. The music and lyrics for the songs were written by Stephen Schwartz, whose credits include *Pocahontas* and *The Hunchback of Notre Dame*. And producer and arranger Hans Zimmer, who also worked on *The Lion King*, composed the instrumentation for the songs and the background music.

"Deliver Us," the first of seven songs in *The Prince of Egypt*, tells the story of Moses' mother putting him in a basket on the Nile and the Queen discovering him. This seven-minute song took six months to complete. "That

"I wanted to express the emotional relationships in the story through the music."
—Hans Zimmer

Hans Zimmer (seated) and Stephen Schwartz work on the music.

A chorus records their part for the song "When You Believe."

song started the whole movie for us," explained director Steve Hickner. "It became crystal clear how we were going to make the picture after that."

"One of the things we set out to do was make sure the songs weren't showstoppers, where somebody just stopped and sang," said director Simon Wells. Rather than bring the action to a halt, the song moves it along. For instance, during "Through Heaven's Eyes," sung by Jethro, Tzipporah's father, the audience sees ten years pass—Moses the prince builds a new life in the desert as a shepherd, falls in love with Tzipporah, and marries her.

"We wanted a song that would embody hope and beauty of the human spirit," said producer Penney Finkelman Cox about the movie's final song, "When You Believe." Penney said the song's inspiration was hatched

when she, Stephen Schwartz, and Steve Hickner were rushing in a jeep through the deserts of Egypt. "We were talking about the need to maintain faith and hope in the face of conflict and difficulty. After the death of the first-

A recording session with the London Philharmonic Orchestra.

born, Moses is shaken by the enormity of what it's taken to free the Hebrews. His sister, Miriam, tries to reassure him by reaffirming their faith in God. This song allows Moses to gather his emotional resources to go on. It conveys the idea that when you believe strongly in something, you find the strength to make it happen.

"We talked about these concepts in lofty and general terms," Penney said. "When I first heard the song, I knew Stephen had managed to capture everything we had talked about that day."

It was Hans's responsibility to take the music and lyrics Stephen created and provide the arrangement for all six songs. This meant deciding which musical instruments he wanted to use, and making sure the musical themes in all the songs were consistent with the feeling of the story. "I wanted to express the emotional relationships in the story through the music," Hans explained. He also wrote the score, or the music that is heard in the background.

Hans Zimmer

 When he was six years old, composer Hans Zimmer wrote a song, which he later used in the movie *Radio Flyer*.

Songs They Sing

In an animated film, it's common practice for a professional singer to provide the character's musical voice. But in *The Prince of Egypt*, four members of the voice cast bravely took on their own singing.

MICHELLE PFEIFFER

Michelle and Sally Dworsky (who sings Miriam's part) sing together in "When You Believe," a moving song about hope and faith.

RALPH FIENNES

Though known for his acting and not his singing, Ralph took voice lessons so he could sing a duet, in a dramatic song about the plagues, with Amick Byram, who provides Moses' singing voice.

STEVE MARTIN
AND MARTIN SHORT

As the two magicians Hotep and Huy, they sing "Playing with the Big Boys," a song in which they boast that their powers are bigger than God's.

Ralph Fiennes, in the recording studio.

Deliver Us

Egyptian guards
Mud . . . Sand . . . Water . . .
   Straw . . . Faster!
Mud . . . And lift . . . Sand . . . And pull
Water . . . And raise up . . .
   Straw . . . Faster!

Hebrew slaves
With the sting of the whip on my
   shoulder
With the salt of my sweat on my brow
Elohim, God on high
Can you hear your people cry:
Help us now
This dark hour . . .

Deliver us
Hear our call
Deliver us
Lord of all
Remember us, here in this burning
   sand
Deliver us
There's a land you promised us
Deliver us to the promised land . . .

Yocheved
Yal-di ha-tov veh ha-rach
Al ti-ra veh al tif-chad
My son, I have nothing I can give
But this chance that you may live
I pray we'll meet again
If He will deliver us

Hebrew slaves
Deliver us
Hear our prayer
Deliver us
From despair
These years of slavery grow too cruel
   to stand
Deliver us
There's a land you promised us
Deliver us
Out of bondage and
Deliver us to the promised land . . .

Yocheved
Hush now, my baby
Be still, love, don't cry
Sleep as you're rocked by the stream
Sleep and remember
My last lullaby
So I'll be with you when you dream

River, O river
Flow gently for me
Such precious cargo you bear
Do you know somewhere
He can live free?
River, deliver him there . . .

Young Miriam
Brother, you're safe now
And safe may you stay
For I have a prayer just for you:
Grow, baby brother
Come back someday
Come and deliver us too . . .

Hebrew slaves
Deliver us
Send a shepherd to shepherd us
And deliver us to the promised land
Deliver us to the promised land

Yocheved
Deliver us!

River Lullaby

sung by Yocheved

Hush now, my baby
Be still, love, don't cry
Sleep like you're rocked by the stream
Sleep and remember
My lullaby
And I'll be with you when you dream

Drift on a river
That flows through my arms
Drift as I'm singing to you
I see you smiling
So peaceful and calm
And holding you, I'm smiling too
Here in my arms
Safe from all harm
Holding you, I'm smiling too

Lu lu lu lu lu lu lu
Lu lu lu lu lu lu lu

Hush now, my baby
Be still, love, don't cry
Sleep like you're rocked by the stream
Sleep and remember this river lullaby
And I'll be with you when you dream
I'll be with you when you dream

All I Ever Wanted

Moses
Gleaming in the moonlight
Cool and clean and all I've ever known
All I ever wanted
Sweet perfumes of incense
Graceful rooms of alabaster stone
All I ever wanted

This is my home
With my father, mother, brother
Oh so noble, oh so strong
Now I am home
Here among my trappings and
   belongings
I belong
And if anybody doubts it
They couldn't be more wrong

I am a sovereign prince of Egypt
A son of the proud history that's shown
Etched on ev'ry wall
Surely this is all I ever wanted
All I ever wanted
All I ever wanted

Queen
This is your home, my son
Here the river brought you
And it's here the river meant
To be your home
Now you know the truth, love
Now forget and be content
When the gods send you a blessing
You don't ask why it was sent . . .

Through Heaven's Eyes

sung by Jethro with the Midianites

A single thread in a tapestry
Though its color brightly shine
Can never see its purpose
In the pattern of the grand design

And the stone that sits on the very top
Of the mountain's mighty face
Does it think it's more important
Than the stones that form the base?

So how can you see what your life is
   worth
Or where your value lies?
You can never see through the eyes of
   man
You must look at your life
Look at your life through heaven's eyes
Lai-la-lai . . .

A lake of gold in the desert sand
Is less than a cool fresh spring
And to one lost sheep, a shepherd boy
Is greater than the richest king
If a man lose ev'rything he owns
Has he truly lost his worth?
Or is it the beginning
Of a new and brighter birth?

So how do you measure the worth
   of a man
In wealth or strength or size?
In how much he gained or how much
   he gave?
The answer will come
The answer will come to him who tries
To look at his life through heaven's
   eyes

And that's why we share all we have
   with you
Though there's little to be found
When all you've got is nothing
There's a lot to go around

No life can escape being blown about
By the winds of change and chance
And though you never know all the
   steps
You must learn to join the dance
You must learn to join the dance
Lai-la-lai . . .

So how do you judge what a man is
   worth
By what he builds or buys?
You can never see with your eyes on
   earth
Look through heaven's eyes
Look at your life
Look at your life
Look at your life through heaven's
   eyes!

Playing with the Big Boys

Hotep and Huy
By the power of Ra . . .
Mut, Nut, Khnum, Ptah,
Nephthys, Nekhbet, Sobek, Sekhmet,
Sokar, Selket, Reshpu, Wadjet,
Anubis, Anukis,
Seshmu, Meshkent, Hemsut, Tefnut,
Heket, Mafdet,
Ra, Mut, Nut, Ptah,
Hemsut, Tefnut, Sokar, Selket,
Seshmu, Reshpu, Sobek, Wadjet,
Heket, Mafdet, Nephthys, Nekhbet,
   Ra . . .

So you think you've got friends in high
   places
With the power to put us on the run
Well, forgive us these smiles on our
   faces
You'll know what power is when
   we are done
Son . . .

You're playing with the big boys now
Playing with the big boys now
Ev'ry spell and gesture
Tells you who's the best, you're
Playing with the big boys now

You're playing with the big boys now
You're playing with the big boys now
Stop this foolish mission
Watch a true magician
Give an exhibition how
Pick up your silly twig, boy
You're playing with the big boys now!

Egyptian priests
By the power of Ra
Mut, Nut, Khnum, Ptah
Sobek, Sekhmet, Sokar, Selket
Anubis, Anukis
Hemsut, Tefnut, Meshkent,
   Mafdet . . .

Hotep and Huy
You're playing with the big boys now
You're playing with the big boys now
By the might of Horus
You will kneel before us
Kneel to our splendorous power . . .
You put up a front

You put up a fight
And just to show we feel no spite
You can be our acolyte
But first, boy, it's time to bow
(Kowtow!)
It's your own grave you'll dig, boy
You're playing with the big boys
Playing with the big boys
Now!

The Plagues

Chorus
Thus saith the Lord:
Since you refuse to free my people
All through the land of Egypt . . .

I send a pestilence and plague
Into your house, into your bed
Into your streams, into your streets
Into your drink, into your bread
Upon your cattle, on your sheep
Upon your oxen in your field
Into your dreams, into your sleep
Until you break, until you yield
I send the swarm, I send the horde
Thus saith the Lord

Moses
Once I called you brother
Once I thought the chance to make
   you laugh
Was all I ever wanted . . .

Chorus
I send the thunder from the sky
I send the fire raining down

Moses
And even now I wish that God had
   chose another
Serving as your foe on his behalf
Is the last thing that I wanted . . .

Chorus
I send a hail of burning ice
On ev'ry field, on ev'ry town

Moses
This was my home
All this pain and devastation
How it tortures me inside
All the innocent who suffer
From your stubbornness and pride . . .

Chorus
I send the locusts on a wind
Such as the world has never seen
On ev'ry leaf, on ev'ry stalk
Until there's nothing left of green
I send my scourge, I send my sword
Thus saith the Lord!

Moses
You who I called brother
Why must you call down another blow?

Chorus
I send my scourge, I send my sword

Moses
Let my people go

Moses and Chorus
Thus saith the Lord

Rameses
You who I called brother
How could you have come to hate me
   so?
Is this what you wanted?

Chorus
I send the swarm, I send the horde . . .

Rameses
Then let my heart be hardened
And never mind how high the cost may
   grow
This will still be so:
I will never let your people go . . .

Chorus
Thus saith the Lord:

Moses
Thus saith the Lord:

Rameses
I will not . . .

Moses, Rameses, and Chorus
Let your (my) people go!

When You Believe

Miriam
Many nights we've prayed
With no proof anyone could hear
In our hearts a hopeful song
We barely understood
Now we are not afraid

Although we know there's much to fear
We were moving mountains
Long before we knew we could

There can be miracles
When you believe
Though hope is frail
It's hard to kill
Who knows what miracles
You can achieve
When you believe
Somehow you will
You will when you believe

Tzipporah
In this time of fear
When prayer so often proved in vain
Hope seemed like the summer birds
Too swiftly flown away
Yet now I'm standing here
With heart so full I can't explain
Seeking faith and speaking words
I never thought I'd say

Miriam and Tzipporah
There can be miracles
When you believe
Though hope is frail
It's hard to kill
Who knows what miracles
You can achieve
When you believe
Somehow you will
You will when you believe . . .

Hebrew children
A-shi-ra l'A-don-ai ki ga-oh ga-ah
A-shi-ra l'A-don-ai ki ga-oh ga-ah
Mi-ka-mo-cha ba-elim Adonai
Mi-ka-mo-cha ne-dar-bu-ko-desh
Na-chi tah v' chas-d'-cha am zu ga-al-ta
Na-chi-tah v'-chas-d'-cha am zu ga-al-ta
A-shi-ra, a-shi-ra, a-shi-ra . . .

Hebrews
There can be miracles
When you believe
Though hope is frail
It's hard to kill
Who knows what miracles
You can achieve
When you believe
Somehow you will
Now you will
You will when you believe

Miriam and Tzipporah
You will when you believe

CREATING THE DESIGN

Art can be a powerful storytelling tool. The images in *The Prince of Egypt* tell volumes about the settings and characters that are not conveyed by either dialogue or music. For instance, the scorching colors and coarse the desert scenes was inspired by the loose impressionism of French artist Claude Monet. The palace design was influenced by the precise and detail-oriented style of nineteenth-century illustrator Gustave Doré. And

Kathy Altieri   Richie Chavez   Darek Gogol

textures of the desert reflect the rough lives and bright hope of the Hebrews, while the elegant, majestic palace celebrates the splendor of Egypt with its mighty pharaohs.

It was up to the art directors, Kathy Altieri and Richie Chavez, and the production designer, Darek Gogol, to create the look of *The Prince of Egypt*. They achieved this by carefully choosing the colors and lighting for each scene and designing the buildings and settings where all the action takes place. For inspiration, they studied works from the classic masters. The look of legendary filmmaker David Lean's work (*Lawrence of Arabia*, *Doctor Zhivago*, and *A Passage to India*) was the influence for the grand scales and epic landscapes of *The Prince of Egypt*.

In the beginning, after almost a year of research, the trio took an eye-opening field trip to Egypt. "To actually be there in person reconfirmed a lot of what we thought Egypt looked like," Richie said. Added Kathy: "It was helpful in that we got to see the colors of the hieroglyphs and some of the Egyptian decorations."

When they returned, they each went about their

specific design tasks: Kathy created the color palettes used in every scene; Richie designed the natural environments: the desert, Midian, and Goshen where the Hebrews live; and Darek designed the architecture of Egypt.

"We wanted the overall design to have the same dignified tone as the story did," Kathy explained. "Because it's a serious story, the colors couldn't be too exuberant."

Several classic works inspired the look of the film, including Bridge Over a Pool of Water Lilies *by Claude Monet (above left), a nineteenth-century Bible illustration by Gustave Doré (above right), and a sweeping vista from* Lawrence of Arabia, *directed by David Lean (below).*

It took 400 artists 3½ years to complete *The Prince of Egypt.*

31

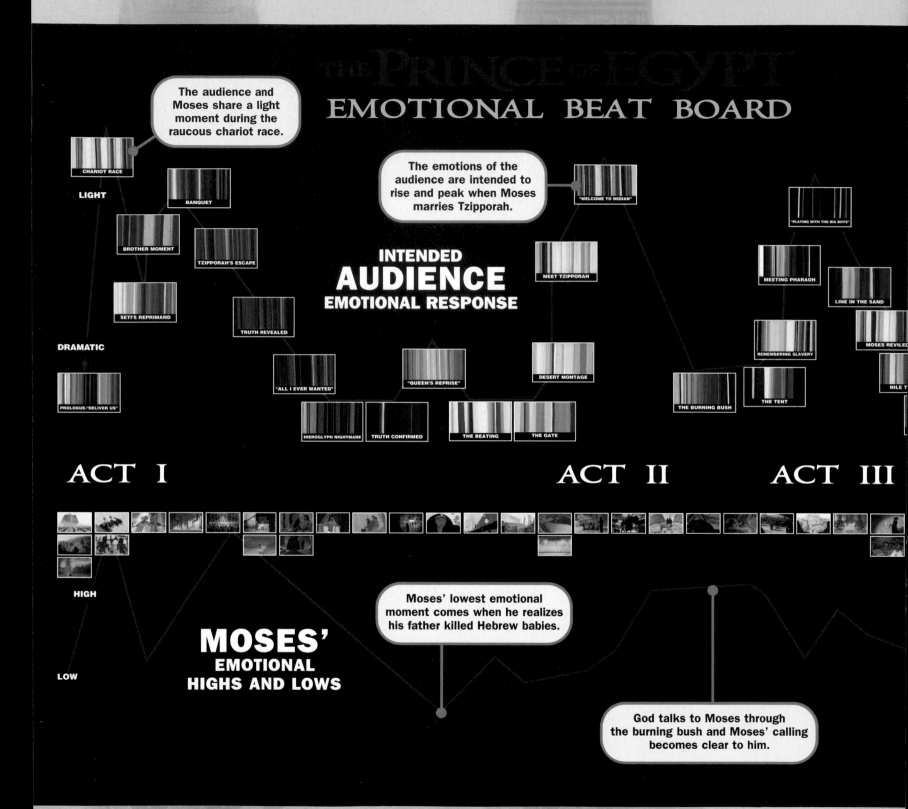

THE PRINCE OF EGYPT
EMOTIONAL BEAT BOARD

The audience and Moses share a light moment during the raucous chariot race.

The emotions of the audience are intended to rise and peak when Moses marries Tzipporah.

INTENDED
AUDIENCE
EMOTIONAL RESPONSE

LIGHT

DRAMATIC

CHARIOT RACE

BANQUET

BROTHER MOMENT

TZIPPORAH'S ESCAPE

SETI'S REPRIMAND

TRUTH REVEALED

PROLOGUE-"DELIVER US"

"ALL I EVER WANTED"

HIEROGLYPH NIGHTMARE

TRUTH CONFIRMED

"QUEEN'S REPRISE"

THE BEATING

THE GATE

"WELCOME TO MIDIAN"

MEET TZIPPORAH

DESERT MONTAGE

"PLAYING WITH THE BIG BOYS"

MEETING PHARAOH

LINE IN THE SAND

MOSES REVILED

REMEMBERING SLAVERY

THE TENT

NILE T

THE BURNING BUSH

ACT I

ACT II

ACT III

MOSES'
EMOTIONAL
HIGHS AND LOWS

HIGH

LOW

Moses' lowest emotional moment comes when he realizes his father killed Hebrew babies.

God talks to Moses through the burning bush and Moses' calling becomes clear to him.

32

The film's highest emotional moment occurs with the parting of the Red Sea and continues through to the end.

EPILOGUE

"WHEN YOU BELIEVE"-Part Two

"WHEN YOU BELIEVE"

RED SEA

The Angel of Death scene is depicted only in black, white, and red.

PERMISSION TO LEAVE

GOD'S WARNING

ULTIMATUM (HALL OF LIFE)

DEATH OF FIRST BORN

ACT IV

Moses hits another high point when, through God, he turns the Nile to blood.

Moses' last emotional low point comes when he sees Rameses with his dead son.

PERMISSION TO LEAVE

The selection of colors for each scene was influenced by the emotional tone of that scene, as shown on an emotional beat board. Drawings from the four acts of the movie were tacked up onto the beat board with a line, curving up and down, indicating the movie's intended emotional impact on the audience. A second line indicates Moses' emotional high and low points. In the middle, a color chart shows the colors selected to match the emotion of each scene. For example, at the movie's darkest point, when Rameses' son is killed, the film became monochromatic—mostly shades of black and white.

These environments—the backgrounds—were created separately from the characters and later joined together. Before the backgrounds were painted, the layout artists did a series of drawings showing what the environments would look like and how the characters would move through each scene. The background artists then painted the backdrops for every scene in the movie, using the colors and styles selected by the art directors. For *The Prince of Egypt*, the background artists painted more than one thousand individual pieces of artwork!

The character designers researched and created every character in the movie. They decided to elongate the characters' faces in *The Prince of Egypt*. The typical face in an animated film is divided into thirds, with each section roughly the same size. To make the characters in *The Prince of Egypt* look more unique, their faces were drawn with the middle section slightly larger than the upper and lower sections.

Moses' face—traditional animation proportions (left), and as it was designed for The Prince of Egypt *(right).*

Once the character designers had created the rough models, the designs were passed on to the animators for further refinements. The character designers then colored and costumed the drawings.

At this point, a maquette (a small statue) was sculpted of each character so the animator could see how it looked in three dimensions. While drawing, the lead animators kept their characters' maquettes close to use as reference.

A background painting.

A maquette, or small statue, was sculpted
of each character so the animator could see how
it looked in three dimensions.

Egypt Field Trip Photo Journal

Simon Wells returns from seeing the sunrise at Mount Moses.

Richie Chavez, Kathy Altieri, and Brenda Chapman visit the Sphinx and Great Pyramid.

Simon Wells and Brenda Chapman take a moment to capture the scale of the Sphinx.

Jeffrey Katzenberg and Darek Gogol sit in front of the Colossi of Memnon, at the mortuary temple of Amenhotep III.

Director Simon Wells poses in front of the step pyramids in Sakarra.

These columns helped inspire the design of the hieroglyphs in the film.

Sandra Rabins and Lorna Cook take a ride on a camel at the Giza Plateau.

The DreamWorks team gets a look at the statue of Rameses the Great at Memphis.

Costume Designer

To maintain the film's historical accuracy and realism and to create the beautiful and detailed wardrobes for the characters, *The Prince of Egypt* had its own costume designer. This is very unusual for an animated movie.

Designer Kelly Kimball's background is in traditional costume design, and this was her first animated movie experience. "But I grew up in a family that was involved in animation, so I knew some of the basics. For instance, in animation, you avoid using a lot of patterns because patterns are too difficult to draw over and over again." But, for the most part,

designing a wardrobe for *The Prince of Egypt* was pretty similar to designing for a live-action film. To get the characters' wardrobe exactly right, Kelly did a lot of historical research. "My two main rules were absolutely no faceted gemstones, because they didn't have them in those days, and no trousers, because they hadn't invented the crotch seam yet. The men wore billowy pants or kilts."

MOSES

GOLD BAND CROWN
WIG
PLAIN GOLD BROAD COLLAR
BRACELETS OF GOLD
DON'T FORGET FINGER RINGS
BELT
SHORT KILT
ANKLETS
BARE FEET
CHARIOT RACE
KELLY

MOSES

EYE MAKE UP
GOLD URAEUS
"WIG COVER" (SHORT VERSION)
GOLD BRACELETS AND ARM BANDS
FANCY BROAD COLLAR
DON'T FORGET FINGER RINGS
BELT
CEREMONIAL APRON
SHORT KILT
ANKLETS AND BARE FEET
BANQUET
KELLY

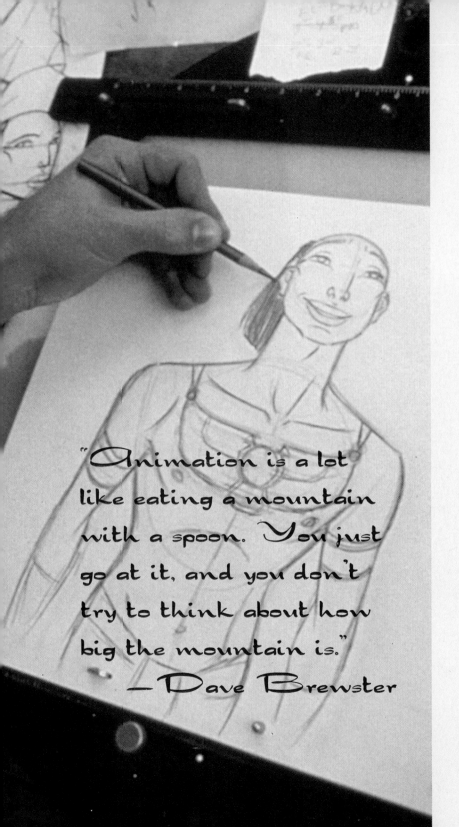

"Animation is a lot like eating a mountain with a spoon. You just go at it, and you don't try to think about how big the mountain is."
— Dave Brewster

THE
ANIMATORS

Let the acting begin. Animators are sometimes referred to as "actors on paper." It's their job, using pencil and paper, to make the characters come alive. They need to be able to realistically depict different types of body movements and facial expressions. One animator reveals that, in order to create a realistic motion on paper, "sometimes we close our doors and start acting out the scenes before we sit down to draw them."

Lead animators supervise a team consisting of anywhere from three to thirty-five artists. The team is assigned a character—sometimes more than one—and they draw every scene that their character appears in. Often, an animator is assigned a character that matches his or her personality and work style. Director Steve Hickner gave this example: "To draw the older Moses, I knew I needed an animator who was an exceptional actor and draftsman, and who could work with a large crew." This is important because the older Moses is in a lot of scenes in the movie and required thousands of drawings.

Because there are so many drawings to be done, animators need to be skilled at drawing quickly. There are twenty-four frames (pictures) per second of film, and each frame requires a drawing. One animator averages forty-eight drawings per week, which translates to only *two seconds* of film. Two seconds a week!

A job in animation may sound like fun, and it is! But it's also a lot of hard work. *The Prince of Egypt* animators, the best in their field, worked for about a year and a half, usually ten hours a day, six days a week.

KRISTOF SERRAND

COMES FROM: Paris, France
ANIMATED: older Moses, Seti
DESCRIBE OLDER MOSES: "In order to age Moses, I gave him long hair, a beard, and wrinkles. Sometimes I just looked at myself in the mirror."

THROUGH THE LOOKING GLASS: "When I'm drawing, I keep a mirror in front of me, and I make faces and draw them. Sometimes I ask a friend to act out scenes for me, so I can make sketches of them."

FAVORITE P.O.E. SCENE: "The one where Seti reprimands Moses and Rameses after their chariot race. I tried to portray Seti as more like a father than a pharaoh."

DAVE BREWSTER

COMES FROM: Ontario, Canada
ANIMATED: older Rameses, the Queen
HOW BAD IS RAMESES? "I can't even say he's a villain. He really does love Moses and tries to keep him from leaving the palace. No one in this film is perfect, and I like that."
LIKE BROTHER, LIKE SISTER: "I don't have any brothers, but my sister and I hated each other growing up. She would always get me in trouble, but now she's my best friend. For Moses and Rameses, I drew from my own experiences of sibling rivalry and love."
A CONFESSION: "I seem to draw women well. I'm not sure why. I've never even been in a dress."

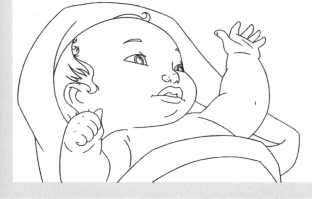

SERGUEI KOUCHNEROUV

COMES FROM: Kiev, Ukraine

ANIMATED: baby Moses, young Rameses

COMING TO AMERICA: "Disney had a competition and I sent in a drawing of Mickey Mouse. They chose me, two people from Croatia, and one from Russia to come work for Disney."

TINY SECRET: "When I started drawing baby Moses, who is about three months old in the film, my own daughter was also three months old. So I just watched her and drew baby Moses."

WHEN THE CURTAIN CLOSES: "I hope the audience walks away from this movie with a feeling they've seen a miracle."

WILLIAM SALAZAR

COMES FROM: Corsica, France

ANIMATED: young Moses

FAVORITE ANIMATED FILM: *Bambi*

YOUNG MOSES: "Moses is a guy who really wants to have fun. He's not like his brother Rameses, who has to carry the weight of being the next ruler. Moses is more carefree—until the moment he discovers who he is and everything changes."

A LITTLE INSPIRATION: "I believe if you really want to do something, you can achieve it. I come from a very small island. There were no jobs in animation there whatsoever. People didn't even know what animation was."

THE FINISHED WORK: "Sometimes I see my work on-screen and say, 'I know this is animation, but I should have made the movements a little bit more fluid.' This was especially important for *The Prince of Egypt*, which is quite realistic. You cannot have Moses jumping around like Roger Rabbit."

Seq 35/sc (19)

RODOLPHE GUENODON

COMES FROM: Paris, France
ANIMATED: Tzipporah
GOT STARTED: At an animation school in Paris. At twenty, he left school to work on *An American Tail: Fievel Goes West*.
FAVORITE P.O.E. SCENE: "When Moses comes home and tells Tzipporah God has spoken to him. Moses could have appeared like a lunatic to Tzipporah. But then there's an understanding between them. It's a pretty strong moment."
FOR YOUR EYES ONLY: "In the early versions of the script, Tzipporah was very sarcastic. Much more feisty than she is in the final version. Now she's still very strong, but she's not as negative."
DREAM JOB: "Animating. Every movie is a different challenge."

ROBERT SCOTT

COMES FROM: Detroit, Michigan
ANIMATED: Miriam
CARTOON FAN: "I used to watch all of the old cartoons, like *The Flintstones* and *Tom and Jerry*. I drew Woody Woodpecker all the time . . . I'd see him in a scene, quickly try to draw him, and when he'd come back on-screen, I'd try to finish it off."
MOTHER KNOWS BEST: "My mom always encouraged my drawing. She said, 'Well, I saw all those cartoons on TV, and I figured somebody's making them. *Somebody* must be making a living.'"
TOUGHEST P.O.E. SCENE: "The very first thing I animated was the scene where Miriam sees Moses when they're older and says, 'But you're our brother!' That was difficult for me because it was a very intense scene—I was used to drawing films that were more lighthearted."
HERE'S A TIP: "You can't draw everything completely out of your head. You might have to look in the mirror to see how your arm moves and bends to get the realism of the motion."

FABIO LIGNINI

COMES FROM: Rio de Janeiro, Brazil

ANIMATED: Aaron

ON AARON: "He's Moses' blood brother. At first he's afraid and cowardly. Then, after the plagues, he sees that things are starting to look better. He represents the part of the audience who might not believe in Moses and has to be turned around."

THE DAILY SCENE: "Animation involves long hours of drawing and repeating and trying again. But when we watch the finished scene with the dialogue, the music, and the backgrounds, it's worth it—that's where the magic is."

FUTURE ANIMATORS, HEAR THIS: "You should be interested in acting and how people behave and how people move—because animation is half drawing, half acting. You have to think in 3-D terms, even though you are drawing on paper. With animation, you have to be able to turn the character around and know what's on the other side."

PATRICK MATE

COMES FROM: Paris, France

ANIMATED: Hotep and Huy

DESCRIBE THE MAGICIANS: "Hotep is the chubby guy, nervous, with a bad temper. He's the leader of the two. Huy is the tall, thin guy who would like to be the chief but can't."

STEVE MARTIN (HOTEP) vs. MARTIN SHORT (HUY): "I was so amazed by Steve Martin's concentration. He prepares very seriously and he also happens to be a great singer. Martin Short is more like a show guy, an extrovert."

STAND-UP ANIMATOR: "My characters were fun to animate. They don't do slapstick, yet their acting was the most comedic. At times they would dance."

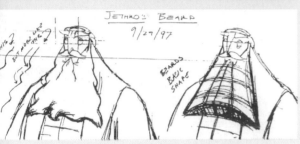

JETHRO'S BEARD
9/27/97

GARY PERKOVAC

COMES FROM: San Diego, California

ANIMATED: Jethro, Tzipporah's sisters

KINDERGARTEN ARTIST: "The teacher would tell us how to draw a tree with a circle for leaves and two lines for the trunk . . . and a big black hole for where the owl lives. I thought to myself, that's not how a tree looks, and I did it my way. The teacher looked at it and said 'that's pretty good.'"

COLLEGE FILMMAKER: "I studied everything about film. Then I took a small animated-film class and spent a year making a film. It was the best thing I did in college."

DANNY GLOVER AS JETHRO: "Danny has very kind eyes and a tremendous smile. You may not see the specific expression, but you can see the same emotion in Danny and Jethro."

RICK FARMILOE

COMES FROM: Santa Rosa, California

ANIMATED: the camel

PEANUTS! "Charles Schulz, Charlie Brown's creator, was an inspiration to me. I think I was in high school when I took my portfolio to Charles Schulz. He looked at it and told me who to contact. That's how I found out what classes to take in college and how to learn about being an animator."

ABOUT THE CAMEL: "He had to be like a real camel, because he doesn't talk. But he's not just a wooden character. I tried to give him personality and make him move a certain way that's humorous without being goofy."

How to Draw Moses and Tzipporah

Moses

#1 Draw a circle. Draw eyes about halfway down circle. Draw lower portion of face.

#2 Add details to eyes and eyebrows. Fill in nose, mouth, and chin as shown.

#3 Draw outline of beard and fill in shading. Add hair.

Tzipporah

#1 Draw a circle. Draw eyes about halfway down circle.

#2 Trace line of forehead at hairline. Draw lower portion of face.

#3 Place nose and mouth as shown. Draw two ovals hanging down from earlobes. Draw hair past hairband. Make sure hair covers ears.

#4 Draw neck and shoulders. Add details to eyes, nose, mouth, and earrings.

Animators' Top Ten

Here are some tips for young animators, from *The Prince of Egypt*'s animation team.

1. Draw what you know and what you like to draw. And draw a lot.

2. Experiment with drawing new things. If most of your sketches are of superheroes, try drawing a landscape or a bowl of fruit for a change.

3. Don't limit yourself with your drawing tools. Draw with anything you can get your hands on: pencils, crayons, paints—acrylics and watercolor.

4. Participate in art classes or special art projects at school. Try different varieties of art, like sculpting clay or even drawing in sand.

5. Practice sketching real-life models. Have a friend or family member sit still while you draw him or her. This exercise, called *life drawing*, is used to train many animators.

6. Tell your parents and teachers that you are interested in becoming an artist. If they know that you're serious about it, they'll be more likely to support you.

7. Take acting or drama classes. Being an animator means being an actor, because you have to understand how people move in order to capture these movements on paper.

8. Observe people—how they smile, how many steps it takes them to get from one point to another, and so on. Imagine that you're freeze-framing every move a person makes and drawing them as separate images.

9. Use a camcorder to make a home video of a person in motion and play it back at a slow speed. Notice all the different motions that go into a seemingly fluid movement.

10. Study animated films. Discover what makes them bad or good. Look at the quality of the backgrounds. See if the drawings have consistency in all the scenes.

Final Line Animators

Once the animators completed their drawings, the drawings went to final line animators, whose job was to clean up the rough drawings.

Judy Howieson, who cleaned up young Rameses, explained her work this way: "I redraw the animators' rough sketches and produce final drawings that are sent to be colored on computer by a computer artist."

For *The Prince of Egypt*, realism and consistency in the drawings were extremely important. "Everyone tends to draw differently," Judy said. "And there can be five to ten animators working on a single character. What I do is make sure a character stays on model [true to the character's design] without losing the animation style that's been created."

What might an animator do that needs to be fixed? "Let's say the character's neck was drawn too long. The easy answer is for me to draw his head lower down. But when the character is moving through the scene, I have to make sure I don't lose the action the animator intended."

Speed, accuracy, and drawing talent are the most important qualities for a final line animator. "I'm a fast worker," Judy said. "But," she added, "you sit drawing all day long. It's just you, a paper, and a pencil. It can be a lot of strain on your hands."

It's important to remember that it's the final line animators' final drawings that end up on the screen, so they have to be flawless. "Without the animators, we wouldn't have our work," Judy said, "but without us, they wouldn't have their product on the screen."

A rough and a cleaned-up drawing of Rameses.

51

SPECIAL EFFECTS

Computer artists used behavioral software to replicate this character many times.

Experts in special effects teamed up with the best traditional animators to create more special effects for *The Prince of Egypt* than for *any* other animated movie to date.

To create a special effect, traditional artists do some of the work by hand, while computer artists do the rest. The DreamWorks computer artists created the big scenes that would be impossible to draw by hand—like the Exodus scene, which depicts one hundred thousand families leaving Egypt, the chariots in Moses' and Rameses' action-packed race, the burning bush scene, and the complex plague sequence. These scenes contain a lot of movement or multiple characters and objects, which would take an animator months, or even years, to draw by hand.

To create the huge crowd in the Exodus scene, *The Prince of Egypt*'s computer artists used state-of-the-art behavioral software, a computer program that can actually duplicate and program characters and objects to behave a certain way. The computer artists entered images of twenty to thirty different people into the computer and programmed it to replicate these shapes into hundreds, even thousands, of people—all of different sizes and colors, and wearing different clothes! The program could also make a character move around an obstacle, such as a rock, in his or her path—or even slow down or change course to avoid another character. The animators triumphed with this new technology. It's nearly impossible to tell the hand-drawn people from the computer-generated ones.

Behavioral software was also pivotal for the plague sequence. There were seven million locusts in one of the plague shots, for instance. It would take much too long for animators to draw that many locusts by hand. So a traditional artist illustrated five to ten drawings of a locust, showing its wings in different positions in order to create the effect of wing-flapping and movement. Then, using the software, the computer artist replicated the

locust drawings seven million times, slightly altering each one's size, color, and movement (for instance, they programmed some locusts to fly in a big broad arc).

Using another revolutionary new computer program developed by the DreamWorks animation team, *The Prince of Egypt* animators were able to create complex action scenes involving a lot of movement. To create the effect of a three-dimensional world, each element— whether a background painting, character, or object—

needs to be able to move independently. The new program, called an exposure tool, allows the computer artists to pull all the elements together and to choreograph all the moves at one time, within a unified environment.

"This is especially valuable for filming action sequences," said scene plan supervisor David Morehead. "The 'camera,' or viewpoint, can move within the actual environment the artists have created. For instance, in the fast-moving chariot race between Moses and Rameses,

This visual development painting was used as reference for color, lighting, and texture for the Red Sea scene.

This computer display shows the water walls, rocks, and crashing waves as they were modeled and animated in 3D.

Textures and lights are added to the 3D surfaces. The textures "etch away" part of the 3D surface to create more organic shapes.

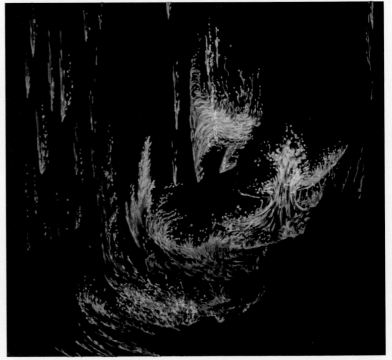

Traditional pencil drawings are created to add splashes and enhance the effect. Color is applied to the drawings in the computer to match the lighting of the 3D images.

The final composite, incorporating traditional drawings and cutting-edge technology.

the camera could pull back or close in on the action as the two chariots charged up and down sand dunes."

The special-effects artists didn't just work on the plagues, miracles, and action sequences. They were also responsible for placing everything that moves, besides the characters, into every scene—including shadows, highlights, and subtle things like smoke and dust. These details add layers of depth and realism to the movie.

The special effects in *The Prince of Egypt* rival the effects seen in the best live-action films. There are actually more special effects per minute of screen time than in any film ever made, whether live action or animated. For the climactic Red Sea sequence, the producers hired special-effects master Henry LaBonta, a top expert in live-action effects, who created the tornado effects in *Twister*. He led a twelve-person team that worked for

more than three years on the four-minute Red Sea sequence. In order to finish it in time, all the computers assigned to the Red Sea team logged a total of 318,000 hours (that's 19 million minutes!) of work.

"At first we had to do a lot of research. We looked at ocean photographs. Then we had to figure out how the actual parting happens," Henry said. "For the close-up splashes, we used handmade drawings, but to make the Red Sea look a mile deep, we created a lot of tiny details that could only be achieved on computer.

"*The Prince of Egypt* is the ultimate special-effects animation film if there ever was one," Henry continued. "Normally, you're creating an explosion or some incidental effect. But in *The Prince of Egypt*, we were creating the character of God—the hand of God's effect on nature—which was pretty exciting."

background overlays

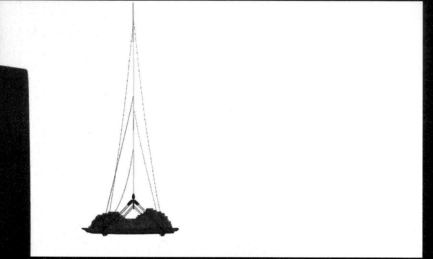

props

BRINGING IT ALL TOGETHER

From this point on, all the work on *The Prince of Egypt* became a digital effort—all the remaining work was done on computer. The final hand-drawn material—the final line animators' drawings and the background art—were all scanned into the computer, and the special-effects department added the effects. Next, a color artist, on computer, added color to the cleaned-up character drawings in each frame. This process is time-consuming, because the colors change in brightness according to the time of day a scene takes place. A color also gets darker if a character moves into a shadow, for instance.

Once the color was added, all the pieces—the special-effects sequences, the painted backgrounds, and the colorized characters—all went to the checking department where everything was digitally combined.

Now that the product was complete, the next step was taking it to the audience. The marketing department produced movie posters and coordinated the newspaper, TV, and radio advertisements. They organized the world-wide release of *The Prince of Egypt*, which means your neighborhood theater first showed the movie at around the same time audiences in England, France, Germany, Italy, Korea, Spain, Sweden, and other parts of the world saw it.

Belief, faith, dreams, hope, promise, and persever-ance—this is what it took for Moses to free his people, and it is also what it took the multitalented cast and crew to create *The Prince of Egypt*.

light rays

special effects—dust

final composed image

The Ten Plagues

One of the biggest challenges for *The Prince of Egypt* team was deciding how to handle the ten plagues. They chose to present a dramatic montage of song, images, and special effects. According to the Bible, these are the plagues that God brought onto Egypt to force Rameses to let the Hebrews go.

1. BLOOD

All the water in Egypt turned to blood—including rivers, streams, and even the water in wooden buckets and stone jars. For seven days, the Egyptians were without fresh water to drink or bathe in. The fish in the Nile River died, and a horrible odor covered the land. But Pharaoh remained steadfast in his refusal to let the Hebrew people go.

2. FROGS

Next, the Nile River became filled with frogs. The frogs jumped out of the river and invaded the palace, the houses, and the streets. Pharaoh begged Moses to get rid of the frogs and promised to allow the Hebrews to make sacrifices to God. But after Moses asked God to kill the frogs, Pharaoh's heart hardened and he refused to set the Hebrews free.

3. GNATS

The dust on the ground turned into nasty gnats. (Some translations of the Bible say this plague was lice, and others say vermin.) At this point, even the magicians believed it was God behind the plagues, but Pharaoh still wouldn't listen.

4. FLIES

Millions of flies swarmed into the palace and throughout Egypt. The land was ruined by these flies. Moses asked Pharaoh to allow the Hebrews to take a three-day journey into the desert to pray and Pharaoh agreed. When the flies were gone, Pharaoh once again went back on his word.

5. DEATH OF LIVESTOCK

Cattle, horses, donkeys, camels, goats, and sheep belonging to the Egyptians all died, while the animals belonging to the Hebrews lived. Yet Pharaoh remained hard-hearted and would not listen to Moses.

6. BOILS

Moses took handfuls of soot from a furnace and tossed them into the air, and a fine dust covered all Egypt, causing painful boils on the Egyptians' bodies. Even the palace magicians' bodies were riddled with painful boils. But Pharaoh continued to refuse Moses.

7. HAIL

Moses stretched his hands toward the sky and rocks of ice fell on Egypt. Hail beat down on the people and the fields of Egypt, destroying all its crops, but did not touch the land of Goshen, where the Hebrews lived. This time Pharaoh told Moses that the Hebrews could leave. Once more, when the rain, hail, and thunder stopped, Pharaoh went back on his promise.

8. LOCUSTS

Locusts invaded Egypt and ate everything that remained in the fields and all the fruit on the trees. At first, Pharaoh seemed finally broken by this plague, but after the locusts disappeared, he once again refused to let the Hebrews go.

9. DARKNESS

Darkness spread over Egypt, and for three days the Egyptians could not see each other or leave their homes.

Pharaoh told Moses the Hebrews could leave but must leave their livestock behind. Moses insisted the livestock must go with them, and an angry Pharaoh banished Moses from the palace.

10. DEATH OF THE FIRSTBORN

Moses told the Hebrews the Angel of Death would come and strike down every firstborn Egyptian. In order to keep the Hebrews safe, they were instructed to take blood from slaughtered lambs and put it on the sides and tops of their doorframes as a sign for the Angel of Death to pass over them. That night, all of Egypt's firstborn died, including the Pharaoh's own son. After this final and most devastating plague, Pharaoh told Moses that the Hebrews had his permission to go.

THE STORY CONTINUES

After crossing the Red Sea, the Bible tells us, the Hebrews embarked on a difficult journey that would last many years, across barren desert land with conditions that severely tested their faith in God.

Three months after Moses led the Hebrews out of Egypt, they arrived at Mount Sinai. God called Moses up to the top of the mountain, and forty days later Moses came down with the Ten Commandments.

But while Moses was up on the mountain, the people grew frustrated and tired. They even created and worshipped a golden calf. This was one of many rebellions during the forty years the Hebrews spent wandering in the desert. Their children, who did not grow up as slaves, kept God's laws and were later allowed to enter the Promised Land.

Moses was 120 years old when God showed him the Promised Land from a distant mountaintop. At God's decree, Moses died on the mountain and never entered the land. After Moses' death the people mourned for thirty days. Then their new leader, Joshua, led them across the Jordan river to Canaan, their new homeland.

Glossary

act: A group of scenes that begins when there's a major shift in time or place.

animator: An artist who draws a character for an animated movie.

art director: The artist responsible for the overall look of the movie.

background artist: The artist who paints the art that appears behind the animated characters.

behavioral software: A special-effects computer program that can duplicate and program characters and objects in a scene to behave in a certain way.

character designer: The artist who researches and designs the look of the animated characters.

checking department: The people who digitally combine all the pieces and check that all the individual visual elements fit correctly with one another, both in space and timing.

color artist: The artist who, on computer, adds color to the final drawings.

computer artist: The artist who uses a computer to create special effects.

costume designer: The person responsible for designing the wardrobe for the animated characters.

director: The creative supervisor responsible for everything from camera angles and color choices to supervising the story team, animators, and composers.

emotional beat board: A board where illustrations for the sequences are laid out according to emotional high and low points in the movie.

exposure tool: A scene-planning computer program that coordinates complex individual movements within a scene.

final line animator: The artist who redraws an animator's rough sketches and produces the final drawings that are ready to be colored.

frame: A single complete image in the film. 1/24th of a second.

head of story: The person who oversees the story team in assembling the story for the movie.

layout artist: The artist who designs the composition of a shot, and draws sketches to show how the characters move through each scene.

lead animator: The head of a team of artists assigned to draw a character.

life drawing: A drawing exercise that involves drawing a real-life model.

live-action film: A film using actors and actresses to play roles in real-life settings.

lyricist: The person who writes words for the songs.

maquette: A small statue of a character that enables the animator to see how the character looks in three dimensions.

on model: Following the exact detailed design created for the character.

outline board: A bulletin board showing all the main events in the story, with selected artwork representing each sequence.

producer: The person who oversees the production of the film, making sure the story is followed, deadlines are met, and a budget is adhered to.

producer and arranger (music): The people who oversee the composition and final sound of the songs and score.

production designer: The artist who is responsible for designing the sets and backgrounds where the scenes take place.

scene: Action within the story that takes place in a continuous location in the same period of time.

score: The music that is heard in the background.

script: The manuscript that contains the movie's dialogue and descriptions of the action and where each scene takes place.

sequence: A series of related scenes that comprise one unit in the story, similar to a chapter in a book.

special effects: Everything that moves in a scene, except the characters. This includes shadows, highlights, smoke, and dust, as well as dramatic effects like the parting of the Red Sea.

story artist: An artist who tells the story with sketches.

storyboard: A bulletin board showing a series of small drawings that tell the entire story, organized into sequences.

thumbnail drawings: Very rough sketches.

voice cast: Actors and actresses selected to be the voices of the animated characters.

writer: An individual who tells the story with words in a script.

More Moses Films

The story of Moses has appeared in many forms—books, plays, movies, and television shows. Here are some Moses films you might want to check out at your local video store.

THE TEN COMMANDMENTS
Cecil B. DeMille's silent treatment of the Bible's Book of Exodus (1923).

THE TEN COMMANDMENTS
Cecil B. DeMille tells Moses' story once more, this time with color and sound (1956).

MOSES
Actor Burt Lancaster plays Moses (1975).

MOSES
Ben Kingsley (who also played Gandhi) plays Moses (1996).

Thank you to Scott McPhail and to all the people at DreamWorks who helped with this book, including Kristy Cox, Paul Elliott, Fumi Kitahara, and Anne McGrath. And also to Stefanie Hamlyn, Tracy Tang, Deborah Kaplan, Mike Reddy, and Dena Wallenstein for their contributions.

PUFFIN BOOKS
Published by the Penguin Group
Penguin Putnam Inc., 375 Hudson Street, New York, New York 10014, U.S.A.
Penguin Books Ltd, 27 Wrights Lane, London W8 5TZ, England
Penguin Books Australia Ltd, Ringwood, Victoria, Australia
Penguin Books Canada Ltd, 10 Alcorn Avenue, Toronto, Ontario, Canada M4V 3B2
Penguin Books (N.Z.) Ltd, 182-190 Wairau Road, Auckland 10, New Zealand

Penguin Books Ltd, Registered Offices: Harmondsworth, Middlesex, England

First published in the United States of America by Puffin Books,
a member of Penguin Putnam Books for Young Readers, 1998

1 3 5 7 9 10 8 6 4 2

TM © 1998 DreamWorks
All rights reserved

The Metropolitan Museum of Art, H. O. Havemeyer Collection,
Bequest of Mrs. H. O. Havemeyer, 1929. (29.100.113)
Photograph © 1996 The Metropolitan Museum of Art

"LAWRENCE OF ARABIA"
© 1962, Renewed 1990 Horizon Pictures (GB) Ltd.
All Rights Reserved
Courtesy of Columbia Pictures.

Printed in the United States of America

Sources consulted:
Encyclopaedia Britannica. Chicago: Encyclopaedia Britannica Inc., 1995.
Hahn, Don. *Disney's Animation Magic*. New York: Hyperion, 1996.
The Jerusalem Bible. Fisch, Harold, ed. Jerusalem, Israel: Koren Publishers, 1992.
Konigsberg, Ira. *The Complete Film Dictionary*, 2nd ed. New York: Viking, 1997.
The New Adventure Bible. Richards, Lawrence O., ed. Grand Rapids, Michigan: Zondervan Publishing House, 1994.